The Kingdom of Heart

∽

A PET LOSS JOURNAL

This book belongs to

_____

In memory of

_____

Departed this life: _____

At age: _____

The Kingdom of Heart

A PET LOSS JOURNAL

Honoring

*Erik, Beau Jingles Bear, Misty, Peety, Erin, Spike, Bow, Andy, Trebles
and all animals who have touched and who continue to touch our hearts.*

Copyright © 2005 by Patty L. Luckenbach

DESIGNED BY TRISH WEBER HALL

SPIRITUAL LIVING PRESS
573 Park Point Drive
Golden, Colorado 80401

ISBN 0-9727184-5-1

Library of Congress Control Number
2005925964

The Kingdom of Heart

A PET LOSS JOURNAL

Patty L. Luckenbach, M.A., D.D.

SPIRITUAL LIVING PRESS
Golden, Colorado

DEDICATION

This memorial journal is dedicated to the animal kingdom. All of life is sacred, the minerals, plants, and animals, great and small. We as humans do not have dominance over life. We share in a relationship of respect and love for all forms of life. The animal kingdom is a sacred kingdom of heart.

In this memorial book I share the energy of unconditional love and the infinite presence of the animal kingdom. May we as humans aspire to open our hearts unconditionally, as our animals have opened their hearts to us. When we open our eyes and hearts to feel and see, unconditional love reaches inward and touches the depth of our individual, instinctual, and intuitive natures. The unconditional love from the animal kingdom can open the gate for humanity's realization of our organic divinity as a holy connection with all of life.

With sincere sympathy I offer this memorial journal to comfort you and to honor your loss.

If we could love as our animals have loved us,
this world would be
the Kingdom of Love.

CONTENTS

4. HOW TO CELEBRATE YOUR ANIMAL FRIEND'S LIFE

5. WHEN YOU'RE READY TO RELEASE

FOREWORD

When I was eighteen years old, I received a letter from my father. I was a freshman in college a few hours north and receiving mail was a rare and much anticipated event.

The letter began with a newsy account of life at home, dad's precise script flowing across the page. On the second page the tone turned decidedly sad with the news of the passing of the family dog, Buffy, at age thirteen and a half. I was standing in the bustling campus commons, which was whirling with excitement and collegiate activity. I was aware only of my pain.

Nearly my entire conscious life included memories of Buffy. She was my playmate, a perpetual greeter in our home, and my snuggling companion. She was now gone and I was not there.

A few months later I made a trip home for the first time since Buffy died. For the first time in my memory, there was no warm fuzzy nose to greet me and no "thump-thump-thump" of a tail pounding out a welcome. The door swung open freely and the hall was empty.

While I had experienced loss in my life, this was the first loss to create a hole I felt simply could not be filled. Twenty-three years have passed since that day and I can still feel the void.

As I read Dr. Patty's beautiful book, I remembered the loss of Buffy in such stunning detail that it nearly took my breath away. At the time, I didn't know how to grieve, or even that I was allowed to grieve my sweet friend, so I simply tucked all my feelings safely away.

Until today.

With fresh tears, I remember Buffy. With adult eyes that have loved and lost, I see her unquestioning face and unbounded love. I recognize these precious qualities that went unnoticed or unappreciated more often than not when she was present.

As I turn these pages, a million moments replay in my head. I now realize that every single time I entered our home during her thirteen years, Buffy joyfully and lovingly greeted me. Every time. Without exception, She was *always* there with unfettered love and a wagging tail. With the benefit of hindsight, I see Buffy for what she was and is to me, an angel with fur. Buffy has been frolicking in heaven for many years now. Yet, she has also roamed a small place in my heart since the day she died, seeking my peace. This book has allowed me to begin to honor her, to celebrate and appreciate her, to grieve and release her.

Yes, the tears reserved for over twenty years are fresh and plentiful…yet they feel good and right. In fact, they fall gently on the head and soft fuzzy ears of a new pet-angel, Shanna, who snores so sweetly and warms my lap as I write these words. How perfectly ironic.

Thank you, Dr. Patty, for writing this book and giving me a tool to release my dear friend, Buffy. Thank you, Great Spirit, for the gift of unbridled, pure, sweet, joyful love that flows unstopped from our creature friends.

–Elizabeth Cabalka
Author of *Wednesdays at the Fluff 'n' Fold–A Caregiver's Oasis*

PREFACE

It has long been my desire to assist individuals who have experienced the deep pain of the loss of a pet. Through years of grief counseling I have seen the profound loss that occurs when a best pet friend dies and how it can relate to other losses we have experienced. I have dedicated my practice to supporting individual grieving and the greater expansion of soul experienced through the life and passing of one's pet.

INTRODUCTION

Some best friends aren't even human. The loss of an animal companion may be one of the most devastating and painful experiences faced by an animal owner. For many, such a loss is as traumatic as losing a family member or a dear friend and can trigger an intense grieving period.

This memorial journal contains true stories that I have collected to encourage you to leave your heart open to life as you remember and grieve the loss of your animal companion. You might say it is a gift you give yourself. You can move through the book at your own pace, with space available for you to express yourself and to remember and to honor your pet friend. I encourage you to paste photographs or drawings of your pet in the book. Each time you open the book, "listen," and you will discover that your precious friend lives forever within your heart. The pages invite you to explore the process of remembering.

This is a respectful means to remember your pet as well as a way to honor the love you have shared. It has been said, "We grieve because we have loved so much!" As stated in *The Land of Tears Is a Secret Place*, "There is a tightness of heart that we are left with after the experience of loss. The tightness of heart leaves us with an open wound to heal. The wound is the emotional pain of loss. The power to open ourselves to pain and mercy brings renewed understanding of life itself, and consequently compassion for ourselves and others."

I have personally experienced the loss of a precious pet. There was nowhere to go with the deep pain that I was experiencing. People said, "Get over it, it is just an animal." I have worked in the field of pastoral care for over twenty years and I know that the loss of our animal companions triggers other losses that have not been properly grieved and that the loss of a loved one can trigger grieving for an animal companion. Grief is emotional pain. Why do we grieve? Because we have loved so much. The closer the bond and the deeper the relationship we have with our animal, the greater the pain.

When our animal companions die, we grieve; but our society does not give us permission to mourn. Dr. Allen Wolfelt has taught that mourning is taking our grief public. When people die, we celebrate their life at a memorial service or a funeral. If we are fortunate, our support system allows us to continue the process of healing. When our pets die, however, there are no traditions to mark our loss, and we are expected to carry on untouched and with our grief unexpressed.

Our animals find our hearts and climb right in with their unconditional love. They leave footprints upon our hearts in a way no other love does.

WHEN A BELOVED ANIMAL FRIEND DIES

CHAPTER ONE

WHEN A BELOVED ANIMAL FRIEND DIES

CHAPTER ONE

ERIK

It was a surreal dream from which I could not escape. The vet technician had just handed me what essentially was a small cookie tin. As I stared at the vessel that contained the earthly remains of my best friend, the vet tech asked me if I was okay. "It just seems so ironic that Erik loved cookies," I stammered, "and he ended up like this."

Several days earlier, on March 18th, I had said my last goodbye to Erik, our seven-year-old Australian Shepherd mix. It was a decision, and an act, that remains as fresh and painful a wound a year later as it was on that day. The fact that I lost him on his birthday, one day before my own birthday, made it an even more poignant loss.

I adopted Erik from an animal shelter after purchasing a house and finally having a backyard that could accommodate a dog. Erik was an energetic one year old whose previous owners had relinquished him for unknown reasons. When I came across Erik in the shelter, he was a bedraggled pup with kennel cough and facial tumors. Something about his eyes, however, caught my attention and I decided (or perhaps he decided for me) that we would make a good team. He had a look that seemed to say, "Well, I've been waiting for you and now, here you are. Let's go!"

Once I got him home it began to dawn on me why his previous family may have made their decision. He was an inveterate chewer. During our first several months together, Erik tried his skills on furniture, art, clothing, tools, just about anything that he could get his mouth around and his teeth into. I tried all manner of training techniques, from yelling to pleading to bargaining. Nothing seemed to work. Pleading would simply make Erik cock his head in such a way that melted my anger, and bargaining just made me feel silly. Yelling resulted in Erik adopting what I called his "guilty performance," in which he would hang his head and look so sorrowful that I would burst out laughing and forget why I was angry. Eventually, Erik decided that I had gone through enough material loss (and had learned to be much less tied to material goods in the process) and simply stopped chewing stuff.

It was Erik's wonderful ability to be a trickster, teacher, and friend that quickly won my heart and bonded us in friendship. Erik, being the first dog to join my family, taught me how to interact with dogs, how training is a shared learning experience for both human and dog.

It was Erik's gentle interaction with young puppies and his boisterous romping with older dogs that taught me about adapting to changing environments. And it was Erik, who proved to be the world's most patient subject, who helped to awaken my passion for photography.

As I approach the one-year anniversary of Erik's passing, I find that I am still working on his most difficult teaching, that of acceptance and letting go. Erik was diagnosed with an aggressive form of cancer that had invaded his lower jaw and throat. As the cancer continued its lethal progress, the hope for treatment quickly faded. Options included surgical removal of the lower jaw or a difficult regime of chemotherapy, neither of which held much promise for either cure or remission.

Because Erik did not seem to be in any discomfort, I made the decision to forgo these treatments, opting instead for an alternative, non-invasive approach to healing using Reiki and Chinese medicine. My greatest wish was to keep Erik's quality of life as high as possible for as long as possible.

When Erik subsequently lost his eyesight, my already growing sense of guilt peaked. I began to berate myself. "If only I had done more for my friend," I thought, "perhaps he could still see." I felt that his loss of vision may have been the final straw for Erik, and that he would quickly succumb to the combined horror of cancer and blindness. However, Erik was ready with another teaching. My intense feelings of guilt created an almost crippling need to protect Erik from any perceived threat. I installed baby gates throughout the house in an attempt to keep him away from stairs and furniture. After several days of coming home from work to find Erik had jumped over the gates to greet me at the front door, my wife suggested that perhaps I try to take Erik out for a walk. "It'll be good for both of you," she said. Erik's happy relief was almost audible. "I'm just blind," he seemed to say, "not dead." He quickly adapted to this new condition, adjusting his movement by listening to my footsteps and the jingling collar of our other dog, Yoshi.

We continued our walks throughout the winter, Erik weaving slightly as he sought audible cues on when to turn and where to step. He quickly learned new commands such as "uppy-up" to help him negotiate curbs and stairs. I checked in regularly with our vet who was amazed at Erik's continued high spirits and who even suggested that the cancer might just "stall out," leaving my friend blind but otherwise relatively healthy. My guilt was slowly replaced with a small seed of hope.

However, several months later we learned that this path was not one that we would travel. Erik's condition quickly deteriorated. He would only eat if I spoon-fed him or allowed him to eat directly from my hand. He could no longer stand on his own. The moment that I had dreaded for six months had finally arrived. Erik was asking me to help him pass from this world.

My wife drove Erik and me to the vet's office. Since Erik could no longer walk, I carried him in. The vet showed us into a private room where we were allowed time to just be with Erik. I could not think of anything to say. The grief was almost crippling, and I held on to Erik for support. As the vet administered the drugs that would allow Erik to peacefully pass, he lifted his head and kicked my arm as if to say, "Steady on! Everything is going to be okay." He then lowered his head and was gone. Now I have memories, memories that often bring smiles, and occasionally tears. And I have Erik's ashes in a cookie tin, which I think he would find hysterically funny. Perhaps I'll take them to his favorite mountain trail and spread them out where he loved to run. I'll say a few words. "Thanks, friend! Thanks for being such a great teacher!" And I'll leave him a cookie, just in case.

I acknowledge Erik, faithful companion and friend of seven years.
–Bob Krugmire

Erik, photographed by owner Bob Krugmire,
professional animal photographer and illustrator.

ACCEPTING AN ANIMAL'S DEATH

Death is a natural life experience. It is the greatest form of change that we as humans ever anticipate. Science tells us that energy cannot be destroyed and that only the way in which the energy has manifested changes forms. When the animal's body is no longer a suitable vehicle for the life force to reside in, it appears that the life force knows its own reality and moves back into the energy wave.

A friend of mine had a male client who had a problem when his dog of fifteen years died. He wanted to know where his pet was. His grandmother put an ice cube in his hand and told him to go out in the summer sun and when the cube melted to come back in. When he did, she told him that that was where his dog had gone. He was still here, but in a different form. What a wondereful analogy.

But death does not feel natural to most people. It feels terrifying. Most of our lives we use various strategies to avoid our anxiety about death. Terms like "away" or "put to sleep" or "put-down," help us avoid even saying the dreaded words–"death" and "died." When we begin to accept the reality that the transition known as death has occurred, then we begin the process of healing the pain that comes from the loss of a pet.

EUTHANASIA

To euthanize a beloved pet is one of the hardest decisions to make. The euthanasia process involves stepping in and through the fiery hoop of grief. There is the wrestling with the thoughts of our pet's illness and the bargaining and even the denial that our pet will die. In *Surviving the Heartbreak of Choosing Death for Your Pet*, Linda M. Peterson states that the word euthanasia comes from two Greek words, *eu* meaning "well" and *thanatos* meaning "death," literally an easy death or way of dying. Euthanasia is a gentler death for our pet than either death in the wild or a natural death. It is the way our pet can lose consciousness and die swiftly with dignity and without pain. Peterson reflects, "Isn't that the kind of death we all want for our loved ones?"

GRIEF

If you have never gone through the death experience with someone you cared for deeply, you may not know what feelings to expect as you face this unknown experience. There is a constellation of feelings that can be expressed. Please know that emotional pain, known as grief, is different for each person. We all grieve differently. The constellation of feelings may include great anxiety because of not being in control of what is happening. There can be fear of letting go and the shock of deep sadness which can overwhelm us as if we were standing in a heavy rainstorm unable to move in from the cold.

With the pain and shock there is also a spiritual harvest that accompanies all dying and eventually gives meaning to the death. What does spiritual harvest mean? A Sufi master tells the story of a bird flying wildly around the room, frantically trying to break through the walls, never seeing that the window has been open all along. The master claps his hands loudly and shocks the bird. It finds the window and is freed. This story is a great metaphor for the spiritual life. In spite of painful conditions and effects, there is always a truth to be discerned. The greater meaning to the death can be revealed.

Many times one holds on to the emotional pain from other losses. If people who were close to you or beloved pets of yours have died in the past, you may still have grief to express regarding the loss of these relationships. Often the emotional pain has not been effectively expressed and begins to accumulate. You may have feelings about multiple losses to deal with.

I like to give this example: When fishing, a good fisherman will hook on to a stringer the fish that he or she has caught and place them into the pond or lake to keep the fish preserved and fresh. We in our lives have had many relationships that we want to preserve and do not want to lose. We keep the memories of what has been so precious down in the pond of our memory, not wanting to realize that our relationship has died. Not until another loss comes forth do we lift the string of previous losses from the pond of our experience. If we have not had the opportunity to grieve the other losses in our lives, the death of our pet can reveal unfinished grieving for other loved ones.

THE GRIEF WHEEL

Until we know our own brokenness, we know not compassion.

Emotional pain is grief, and grief is a process, a movement. Life, too, is a process and certain things happen at certain points along the way. Many of these things have the capacity to expand our understanding of life.

The grief process begins with shock and inability to absorb reality. Protest, anger, depression and despair, confusion—all are appropriate responses to loss. The process of grieving is not linear. It is circular in nature, and the different feelings associated with loss are at times experienced as a constellation of feelings. There is no set pattern or sequence. Just when you feel you have reached the end of a process, a fragrance, a sound, or a memory can launch the cycle of grieving. But each time you spiral with your feelings of loss, you gain a greater understanding of who you are. You move into a larger self and have a more compassionate understanding of both yourself and others.

A Zen definition of compassion is "understanding the lack of understanding." Life brings forth constant change, and there are times when great meaning is revealed and other times when there is a synthesis of understanding that builds compassion.

The grief wheel on the next page illustrates the phases of grief that we experience.

GRIEF WHEEL • CIRCLE OF LIFE

PROTEST
- Denial
- Unfairness
- Anger
- Shock
- Numbness
- Fear

LOSS

DESPAIR
- Guilt
- Feelings of insanity
- Anger
- Helplessness
- Nothing will be the same

REPASS
Remembrance can re-launch the cycle of Grieving

DETACHMENT
- Decreased Socialization
- Short attention span
- Lack of patience
- Depression

RECOVERY
• Focus on present service • Compassion
• Increased sensitivity • New awareness • Open heart

A PET LOSS LITANY

There are several feelings regarding losing a pet that seem to be universal. The following pet loss litany is adapted from a contribution of the Love is Forever Support Group. Let yourself connect with these feelings that so many of us share.

Guilt

I believe that guilt is a thought that can move in and lodge within us as a feeling. J. Ruth Gendler wrote, "You may recognize guilt's footsteps before you see her coming. She limps like a crippled bird. Even though her broken ankle is healing, the wound in her heart has become infected." Guilt is a self-condemnation that we place upon ourselves.

Guilt is a reflection of never being good enough. Guilt is a lonely dark scary place, and it's hard to find the door. Guilt is being angry with yourself for not being perfect. Guilt is feeling that you should have tried more ways to make things better before resorting to euthanasia. Pet animals cannot speak for themselves and rely on us for their care. Are our decisions for them right?

Guilt is a filter that makes the memory of joy and love not as bright as it's meant to be.

Helplessness

In the process of recovering and adjusting from the loss of our animal we feel the grief, the emotional pain. Helplessness can spring from the process of trying to readjust our lives and to who we are now. It feels like a fish out of water—frustrated that it doesn't grow legs to walk on the land.

Helplessness is being powerless. Helplessness is feeling out of control and unable to handle life.

Helplessness is confusion. We do almost anything to avoid the emptiness of loss because it is so frightening to contemplate. Helplessness is being out of control—my feet in the air.

Helplessness is watching the death tremors of a loved one. The lives and illness and aging of our animals are not all under our control. Helplessness is the feeling that we may have made mistakes or can't fix what's happening.

Love and Companionship

Love is a verb, and it is the self-givingness of life. Our animals unselfishly give to us unconditional love. They do not speak with voice but are our companions, faithful and true. We take care of their basic needs, and they give to us authentic companionship. Love and companionship are the greatest gifts in the world. They are two of the best things about having a pet and two of the worst things we are afraid of losing.

Love and companionship is the wonderful relationship with your pet when you share love unconditionally. Love is the unconditional two-way street between our animal companions and us. Love is a feeling that transcends death and brings hope for a new day.

THE SOUL OF AN ANIMAL

Nature teaches about our organic connections with all of life. The indigenous peoples of this planet have believed that there are seven kingdoms that constitute all of life as we know it. Six of them are the mineral, plant, animal, human, ethereal, and spiritual kingdoms. We are all related; and the seventh kingdom is the realization of our relatedness within our heart center. When we accept each kingdom and sense the matrix of life, then we do not demand dominion over the animals and the earth. Then we have a deep instinctual and intuitive knowing that the kingdom of God holds all of life precious and sacred.

I believe minerals, plants, and animals are of the Love-Intelligence known as God. Therefore, I believe each animal has a soul. All animals are connected to the center of the great circle of life just as we humans are connected to that great circle.

I have been a pastoral care minister for twenty years and have observed many people of all ages die. I believe that when the body is no longer a suitable residence for the soul, the soul, knowing its own immortality, moves from this life dimension to inherit a new form of life. Our transformation or death process is also a birth process; the labor pains of birthing move us into a greater dimension of eternal life. Every life form has a window of departure into the greater dimensions. All animals have this window just as we humans do.

In her book *Conversations with Dog*, Kate Solisti-Mattelon wrote: "Dogs are aware of their connection to God. Unlike most humans, they have never forgotten or lost it." The angels, ascended masters, and even our own soulfulness know of the oneness with God and all other beings. We humans are desperately trying to remember these connections.

Our precious animals live in the present moment and are attuned to their instinctual connection with life. They do not have the ego attachments, acquired beliefs that demonstrate as habit and conditional love, that humans have. Animals help us to connect to our spiritual intuition. So above, so below, they know we live in a field of unity. They are aware of the organic connection to the greater weave and tapestry of life. The animals have not forgotten the kingdom of love for it is their intuition and instinctual birthright to be a part of the greater whole.

Kate Solisti-Mattelon wrote, "The mission of all dogs is to bring unconditional love to humanity through the qualities of loyalty, devotion, and complete acceptance." Therefore, all animals' spiritual practice is compassion and love, joy, and being fully present in the Now.

We as humankind have thought of the animals as separate from us or that their purpose is to just do for us. Their purpose is to be and to serve. As the profoundly meaningful book, *The Legend of Rainbow Bridge* by William N. Britton states, "Our animals wait for us and greet us as we open the gate of heart and move into the greater life." As a minister serving the greater spiritual truth, I am certain that it is not death, but life, that is eternal.

Many pet lovers are familiar with the legend of Rainbow Bridge. According to this story, beloved pets cross a multi-colored bridge to a special land when they leave this earth. There they find a place of lovely weather, wonderful food, and endless fresh water. All the animals are in perfect health and as a playful and spry as ever. The only thing missing from this paradise is the person with whom they were so intimately connected in their former life.

In *The Legend of Rainbow Bridge*, the author describes when one of the residents: "suddenly stops playing and looks into the distance. The bright eyes are intent; the nose twitches; the eager body begins to quiver. Suddenly your pet breaks from the group, flying over the green grass faster and faster.

You have been spotted, and when you and your special friend meet, you cling together in joyous reunion, never to be parted again. The happy kisses rain upon your face; your hands caress the beloved head, and you look once more into those trusting eyes, so long gone from your life, but never absent from your heart.

Then you cross the Rainbow Bridge together, never again to be separated."

THE LANGUAGE OF LOVE

CHAPTER TWO

THE LANGUAGE OF LOVE

CHAPTER TWO

OF MICE AND MEN

Ionce exchanged letters with an inmate of Arizona State Penitentiary. He was on death row and appreciated the connection with the outside world. He shared with me that he had adopted a little gray mouse. The inmate saved crumbs of food to feed his friend, and he shared with me the comfort the mouse brought him.

This man had been an angry giant. He had stepped on everything that had ever gotten in front of him in his life. The effects of his hardened heart had placed him on death row awaiting execution. Now his little mouse friend meant the world to him. The little mouse had a way of opening the inmate's heart with the language of love. It reflected nonjudgmental and unconditional love in the twinkle of its tiny mouse eyes. The little mouse became a part of the dead man's story.

The mouse taught the man a most common and basic truth with an unspoken language of love. Perhaps if all children everywhere could experience unconditional love, our prisons would not overflow with individuals who have fought against life. When there is a morsel of food in our bellies and love in our hearts, we realize we have the keys to the kingdom of heart.

Our rational minds can outline and become controlled by reason and logic, but the animal kingdom only communicates with the language of feelings. The animal kingdom has prospered because the language of feelings knows only the life force that holds the stars in the sky and encircles each of us with the seasons of sun and moon.

Whether the animal is a dog, a cat, an iguana, or a mouse, the language is the language of feelings.

LOSS CAN HAPPEN IN MANY DIFFERENT WAYS

Animals act as our companions, teachers, our children, best friends, and in many cases they hear and see for us. Our domestic animals depend on us for food, water, grooming, and general good care. Every day they are a part of our responsibility. The rewards certainly outweigh the time we spend caring for them.

Many times our first experience with loss is the loss of our pet, and that loss can occur in many different ways. Some pets have to be given away because of changes in life experiences, such as when families move to new apartment complexes that do not allow pets. We've all heard heart-warming tales of dogs and cats that traveled hundreds of miles to find their owners, but it is not always the story that we are reunited with our pets.

Sometimes pets run away…Once I was driving in the high country with friends. It was a windy day. We stopped for a picnic lunch and heard a whimpering in the distance. Investigating, we found a very thin and shivering retriever sheltering from the wind on a bed of dried grass. It looked as though the dog had endured the elements of the mountain for days. We gave her food and water, and I drove the rest of the day with this grateful four-legged passenger. I named her "Windy Day." As I approached the city, I did the responsible thing and called the phone number on her tag. Her owner seemed pleased that she had been found. In my heart I wanted to keep her, for how strong she had been to survive the mountain, and she seemed so grateful to be warm and safe. That day Windy Day and I communicated with heart.

I delivered the dog to her owner, a large man with a firm voice. He yelled at her, and immediately yanked her to discipline her. My heart sank, and I wanted to cry. He didn't say, "Gee, thanks." He just slammed the door. When the wind blows strongly, I think of her and hope the man was only hardening his heart from me and that he allowed Windy Day to keep his heart open to feelings and to a greater love of himself and others.

The breakup of a family can also involve the loss of a pet. When my former husband and I were preparing to separate and divorce, we drew straws for the cat. He won the draw, and it was hard for me to let go of our beautiful black cat, but I realized that it was important that the cat reside with him. It was the cat that touched him at a heart level.

Of course, some animals are killed in accidents. "I chased Gilbert right in front of a city bus." This was Mrs. Olson's dismay and her story. Mrs. Olson was known for giving daily treats to all the animals in her neighborhood. She had a great sense of humor and a big heart and a large pocket filled with treats. The story was passed to new neighbors that Mrs. Olson loved animals but that she had chosen not to have a pet of her own.

Years prior her dog, Gilbert, a wire-haired terrier who loved to run free, had gotten out the front door of her house. In her attempt to get him back into the yard Gilbert ran in front of the city bus that ran along the avenue. Gilbert was killed right before her eyes. She could not endure the pain of losing another animal and chose instead to feed and love the neighborhood pets.

Animals come to us and leave us in many different ways.

My husband Luke grew up on a farm. At age nine, he had a favorite cow-herding dog. Because Luke's dog was not performing as well as the herders, his uncle shot the dog and killed it. Fifty years have passed since his uncle killed his dog, but the image lives on within Luke's heart. He says, "I never liked my uncle after that!"

HOW TO WORK WITH A CHILD WHO GRIEVES THE DEATH OF HIS OR HER ANIMAL

Children have a natural respect for the animal kingdom. Perhaps it is the heart connection that is felt between them. Animals have a playful, humorous aspect, and children naturally relate to kittens and puppies; they experience the simple delight of a lizard sunning on the rocks. You may have heard of the child who insisted that her gerbil be laid to rest in an old matchbox, the box lined with cotton for a pillow. The little children gather, and the matchbox is placed within the earth. The simplicity of the child's heart knows that Mother Earth will cradle her gerbil friend.

Dr. Alan Wolfelt, director of Children's Transitional Center, states, "If a person is old enough to love, he is old enough to grieve." So many times the child is the forgotten mourner. We as adults forget that the child has loved the pet and the pet needs to be honored and remembered.

Assisting children to grieve the loss of animals requires for us as adults to be open and honest about the loss. Do not use phrases such as "he is asleep," "he's gone away" or "he's just resting." Be honest. You can't really fool a child and it is best to let your child know the animal has died. One neighbor's cat was run over by a car, and Billy's mother quickly disposed of the remains before he could see it. After a few days, though, Billy finally asked about the cat. "Bill, the cat died," his mother explained, "but it's all right. He's up in heaven with God." Billy asked, "What in the world would God want with a dead cat?" Be honest. Allow the child to tell stories about the animal. Encourage him to color or draw a picture of the animal and talk about the picture. Storytelling can be healing. Invite the child to plan and participate in a memorial tribute for the animal. Create a simple ritual that honors the beginning and ending of the life cycle. Let children know that it is okay to feel sad about the animal's passing. The only language that was felt between the child and the animals was the language of feelings. Give the message that it is okay to feel.

Grief does not focus on one's ability to understand, but instead upon one's ability to feel. Any child mature enough to love is mature enough to grieve. Be aware that the loss of animals can bring forth a cluster of other losses that were not completely felt and acknowledged. In this way, the loss of an animal can be the catalyst for an opening of our hearts and the transformation of our lives. Our animals continue to be teachers of the heart even after their passing.

HOW TO EXPRESS YOUR
FEELINGS OF GRIEF AND LOSS

∽

CHAPTER THREE

HOW TO EXPRESS YOUR FEELINGS OF GRIEF AND LOSS

᭶

CHAPTER THREE

CANVAS OF YOUR SOUL—GIVE YOURSELF TO JOURNALING

Writing in a journal can be a beautiful therapeutic tool for you in working through your grief. Permit me to say a few words about the tool of journaling (or writing down) your feelings and experiences. You have the freedom to write in your book however you choose. No one is grading it, analyzing it, correcting your spelling, or checking for complete sentences. Here is your opportunity to express your feelings. There is no right or wrong to it! If you don't know how to get started, begin with the present moment or the present period. If you find resistance in writing, just write the word "resistance" over and over again to honor what you are feeling in the present moment. If you proceed this way, I guarantee your heartfulness will break through the resistance.

Journaling as a therapeutic tool provides a way to transmute energy in order to harvest the gifts of grief that move with the cycle of life. It may be helpful to use the empty pages that follow and begin to list your feelings. Journalers refer to this technique as catharsis writing. "Catharsis writing is done under pressure of intense emotion that calls for immediate expression. It could be as simple a statement as 'I'm so depressed!' says Tristine Rainer in *The New Diary*. It provides an emotional release. Put your scream, your tears into your memorial book. I have also provided some completely blank pages in this workbook. Many people find it comforting to illustrate their thoughts and feelings with drawings or photographs. Fill these pages however feels best to you.

The journaling process has been beneficial for me and for countless others in the understanding of and reorientation to life by taking the first step in acknowledging the loss and the pain that comes from losing our most faithful friend, our animal. May this memorial book allow you to loosen the tightness of your heart and to record the precious memories of your pet.

SUGGESTED TOPICS FOR JOURNALING

It is helpful to have what Kay Adams in her book *Journal to the Self* calls a "springboard." The springboard is a word or phrase that helps you to take the plunge into writing your thoughts and feelings. Some of my suggestions include:

- How we found each other
- The guilt I felt in having to put you down
- What I wish I could have told you
- My favorite story about you
- What I loved most about you
- How you feed me
- What I have learned about myself because of you

CANVAS OF YOUR SOUL

Use these pages to express your thoughts and feelings about your pet.

CANVAS OF YOUR SOUL

Illustrate your feelings with photographs or drawings.

A LETTER TO YOUR PET

Another way of experiencing your feelings is to write a letter to your pet. If you like, try starting the letter with one of the following phrases:

• You, my most faithful friend were always…

• You believed in me.

• How I can express my gratitude.

• How I will miss you.

• What you gave to me.

Write a letter to your pet here.

Dear

YOUR ANIMAL FRIEND'S LETTER TO YOU

Some people find it helpful to "hear from" their pet. Maybe you'd like your animal friend to write to you.

Example:

Dear Friend,

    You gave me life when I was old. You loved me, cared for me. I like it at night when you bless me in your prayers. I left so quickly on my last breath, but know that I'm not far from you. Just call my name, and I will come. By the way, when your new puppy, Willie Tall Tail, is chasing his tail, he is really seeing me chasing him.

    Friends forever,
        Beau Jingles Bear

Become quiet. Take a few deep breaths. Turn the page, and write whatever comes to mind.

Dear _____

MY BEST FRIEND

Man's Most Faithful Friend

Bob had experienced diabetes for years, and the disease had taken his eyesight. Bob made his transition and finally reached the gateway of death. His soul, knowing its own mortality, set down the heavy flesh, so that Bob could see now into his greater life.

I was honored to officiate at Bob's funeral service. It was a profoundly moving experience. Bob's guide dog, Sammy, sat in the front row with Bob's family. That alone moved everyone in attendance, but a compassionate series of events unfolded to truly pull on the ropes of my heart.

As people filed by the casket, Sammy sat attentive, very regal and still. The guests slowly moved out of the chapel, and those who were left were Bob's family and Sammy, the funeral director and myself. Family members paid their last respects to the hollow shell of Bob's physical body. Sammy did not move until all had left the casket and were assembling in the chapel. Then, as though Bob was calling him, Sammy broke his regal stance and moved beside the casket. He rose to view his master for the last time. There was not a dry eye in room. Everyone present stood motionless, including the funeral director. All felt Sammy's grief.

At the cemetery I always stay with the funeral director until the family leaves and the grave is attended to. Bob's son and faithful Sammy stayed with us that day. Sammy made sure his master was cared for. It was one a great and profound demonstration of a dog being man's most faithful friend.

MY BEST FRIEND

Use these pages to describe your best friend. Write whatever comes to your mind.

MY BEST FRIEND

Use these pages to illustrate, in whatever way you like, your best friend.

YOU WERE AN ANGEL TO ME

Angel In A Fuzzy Suit

Erin was a beautiful Golden Retriever and a hospice dog who made his rounds daily to check on all the patients at the hospice. The pets that serve to visit people in hospitals and in hospice are special angels dressed in fuzzy suits. Even people who have never had a pet in their life experience comfort in the gentle presence of the animals who serve in this way.

Alice Dole loved her daily visit with Erin; and when her physical condition improved and she was sent home, she missed him. A year passed without the friendly visit from Erin. When Alice's physical condition worsened, she entered the care of another good hospice.

I was called to visit Alice in the new hospice. She was a mere bony frame lying motionless in the fetal position. This once vital woman had shrunk to a small mound on a huge bed. As Alice slipped into a coma, her last whispered wish was to see Erin one more time. Erin had retired as a hospice dog; but his owner was found; and Erin was summoned.

I was present in Alice's room when Erin and his owner arrived. Erin very graciously entered and walked directly to Alice's bed. He stood there for a moment. He surveyed the entire room as though he were seeing other angels. He then moved to the other side of the bed and sensed a place to lie beside Alice. Erin seemed so big compared to Alice's fragile body, but with great respect the dog positioned himself against her. It seemed as though he paced her shallow breathing.

Although Alice had not moved a muscle in weeks, she now reached out her arm to touch and surround Erin. What peace filled the room! Within seconds Alice's breath ceased. She had waited for the fuzzy angel to be by her side.

Erin with his owner was present at Alice's memorial service. I learned just recently that Erin himself had passed on into the greater eternal life. No doubt Alice and many more loving souls were there to greet God's fuzzy angel.

I respectfully honor the service dogs of this world. Thank you Erin!

YOU WERE AN ANGEL TO ME

Do you feel as though your pet was an angel to you? Write about your angel friend on the following pages.

YOU WERE AN ANGEL TO ME

Use this space to draw or place photos of your angel animal.

GIFTS YOU HAVE GIVEN ME

Misty's Gift

My Golden Retriever Misty had been my beloved companion since she was six weeks old. From the moment I laid eyes on her, I felt a deep spiritual connection. She loved life; she loved people; and she followed me everywhere. She had rarely been sick and was always a bundle of energy whether she was running with the horses or chasing the jackrabbits on my ten-acre mini-horse ranch.

When she was five years old, we moved to a smaller home in the suburbs of Denver, and she adjusted quite well. She enjoyed many long walks around the neighborhood and many afternoons doing yard work or playing with her two friends Sonya and Buddy. As she entered her seventh year, she began having seizure-like episodes. Greatly concerned, I took her to my veterinarian who performed a battery of tests. The results were inconclusive, and my vet could not determine the cause of the seizures. Things seemed to settle down the rest of that year. I hoped that maybe Misty's seizures had ended, but one morning at the end of January, she began having a seizure. I rushed to get dressed and drove her the few miles to the vet thinking that if he could observe what was happening it might give him a clue as to the cause. He checked her over carefully and thoroughly, took blood samples, but once again the results were inconclusive.

Misty recuperated quickly and was back to her old self. Then one evening, late in November, she began acting like she was in a lot of pain and could hardly move. I rushed her to the vet and upon examination they determined that her stomach had twisted, and she would have to have surgery or Misty would die. I was frantic with worry and was willing to do whatever was necessary to save her life.

The vet consulted with the Veterinary Referral Hospital of Colorado and after being examined by their doctors, Misty's surgery was scheduled for 3:00 P.M. I left her in their experienced hands and prayed as I waited to hear the results of the surgery. Abruptly the phone rang and Dr. Sims said that as they were intubating Misty for the surgery, they found a large tumor that seemed to be wrapped around her carotid artery. They wanted to know whether or not to proceed. After quickly weighing the pros and cons, I decided to have them fix the stomach and also try to remove the tumor.

The stomach surgery was very successful but the veterinary team was not able to remove the entire tumor. They had nicked a few nerves leaving one side of her face slightly paralyzed. I visited her every day and called several times each day to keep abreast of her progress.

This highly malignant thyroid tumor that the doctors had not been able to find previously was the cause of her seizure-like episodes and her twisted stomach. As it grew, it had slowly begun cutting off her air and blood supply.

On the fifth day after her surgery she seemed well enough to come home. I was very excited and happy as I drove to pick her up. However, Dr. Sims met me at the door with a sad look on her face and told me that Misty had collapsed from pneumonia. I was overwhelmed with the scene before me. She lay under the oxygen tent laboring for each breath. As I approached, she weakly wagged her tail and seemed to relax a bit. The prognosis was not good and with a heavy heart I decided to have her euthanized.

As I tearfully said my goodbyes, I told her how much I loved her and that she would always hold a special place in my heart. I also asked her to come back to me again, whether as another loving animal or as a spirit guide. She passed peacefully, and I could feel her energy with me as I made the long drive home.

It was very difficult to get into the Christmas spirit, but two weeks later I decided to put my Christmas tree up. As I had finished packing away the empty boxes, I noticed something shiny on my couch. I thought it was a piece of tinsel, but to my amazement it was the diamond earring that I had lost! In my hurry and excitement to get Misty to the vet that morning, it had come loose and fallen off. I had searched every nook and cranny in the house, car, and even the vet's office, but had never found it.

This was a miracle! It was truly a *gift* from Misty! She was returning something precious to me as a way of thanking me for the love and care I had showered her with in the wonderful nine years we had shared together. It was also her way of showing me that there is life after death and that she is and always will be a part of my life!

–Sue Tanguay,
Misty's dearest friend of twelve years
Littleton, Colorado

GIFTS YOU HAVE GIVEN ME

Let your animal friend know about the gifts he or she has given to you.

GIFTS YOU HAVE GIVEN ME

In drawings or in photos, illustrate gifts that your pet has given you.

THE HARDEST DECISION I EVER HAD TO MAKE

Peety's Story

Peety, a very high-strung and energetic Bichon Frise, was losing her energy, and Peety's energy is what defined her. She had Cushing's disease, an adrenal disorder that often results in drastic weight changes. Peety was becoming emaciated despite her voracious appetite. Medication for her illness would have put undue stress on her heart, and she was displaying signs of pain, although she would deny that and try to hide it. She was also incontinent and wearing a diaper, which of course, she was not happy about.

I decided that enough was enough. Peety wasn't Peety anymore. Still, I felt a bit guilty about making the decision to have her euthanized. Deep down, I thought, who was I to make such a decision for another being? So I made a few phone calls. The support I received from the community was incredible. I did not realize that such a support existed.

The day before Peety's final appointment, I called again for support. Another compassionate being spent an hour on the phone with me discussing my concerns. She was willing to spend as much time as I needed. I concluded that Peety was trying to tell me that it was time for her to go.

That night I took Peety to our neighbor to say goodbye. The neighbor had a friend visiting who a few days earlier had lost her own little dog, a Maltese named Paki. She hadn't been able to say goodbye properly and asked if she could spend a few moments alone with Peety. She gave Peety a message to give to Paki on the other side. So close to her own end Peety had an opportunity to help heal another dog owner, an important job!

I wanted Peety's last day to be pleasant, so I cancelled any appointments that I had for that day. No diapers on her last day! Bill, my husband, and I took her to Bouton Veterinary Hospital in the late afternoon of a beautiful day in May. The sun was warm; the grass looked greener than normal; and there was a slight breeze. Everything was ready for Peety. We all sat on a blanket under a tree and opened Peety's favorite treat, a can of tuna. We said goodbye and told her to meet Paki on the other side. The vet and vet tech were very warm and supportive. We let Peety wander around for a while on the grass while her sedative took effect. We held her as the final injection was administered, and her heart stopped in less than thirty seconds. I imagined her greeting Paki.

The vet said that if we had not made the decision we did for Peety she may not have died so peacefully. As I walked away and looked back at her little white body lying on the green grass, I had a hard time grasping that she wasn't just taking a nap. I couldn't help but think that that's the way I would choose to make my own transition.

A little while later I received a poem along with a lock of Peety's fur and a card with Peety's name and paw print on it from the vet tech. My neighbor and her friends and Bill and I had a little ceremony to acknowledge the animal spirits in our lives, living and dead, and how they have blessed us. We brought pictures of our four-legged friends and honored them. The ceremony gave me great peace and a sense of Peety's unconditional love.

–Julie Odler,
Peety's best friend
Denver, Colorado

Often, a responsibility of pet ownership is having to decide to euthanize your animal friend. As trying as this decision can be, you know in your heart when it is the right thing to do. The following lines from the unattributed poem *The Last Battle*, are written from the animal's standpoint. To me, they speak to what we must remember:

If it should be that I grow frail and weak,
And pain should keep me from my sleep,
Then will you do what must be done?
For this–the last battle–can't be won…

Although my tail its last has waved,
From pain and suffering I have been saved.

Don't grieve that it must be you
Who has to decide this thing to do.

We've been so close–we two–these years.

Don't let your heart hold any tears.

THE HARDEST DECISION I EVER HAD TO MAKE

Write in the following pages about the difficult decision to euthanize your pet; perhaps one of the hardest decisions you had to make.

A FUNNY STORY ABOUT MY PET

The Cat Burglar

Cats at times seem to be cosmic in nature. They are not saints, but they have been sent to us as a reminder to be light on our feet and to be fully engaged and focused–and to be curious and cute. It has been said that cats have nine lives. So the question is, do their characters jump in and out of their many expressions of life, in one moment appearing to be a saint in a fuzzy suit and in the next moment being sent on a curious mission of intent?

I share the funny story about my friend, Spike, who was sent to me to teach me to stay poised and light on my feet. Spike was a big gray and white tom with an awesome might. From day one he thought he was a dog. He would play fetch and jump high into the air to catch a frizbee. He received his name because his claws were like little spikes. The majority of Spike's day was spent peacefully purring and stretched at the bottom of the bed. I could not imagine what my world would be like without my beautiful and peaceful Spike.

My beloved grandmother had given me an expensive, beautiful diamond ring that had been in our family for years. How proud I was to have this very valuable and brilliant piece of jewelry that had been worn by my ancestors.

One day I noticed the ring was missing. I looked everywhere for it. Spike remained still as I frantically searched for the beautiful and much loved ring.

Days passed. I rehearsed what I would tell my grandmother about the missing diamond ring. Days later I was cleaning out my garage and turned over a bicycle helmet. Inside were not only the missing ring but also several other pieces of jewelry. As I stood in amazement I felt the curious eyes of a cat thief gazing at me in surprise. A gray and white flash dashed from my sight.

Who would have ever thought that peaceful purring Spike had been working the night shift as a cat burglar? I miss my funny friend Spike, and I realize that he was indeed a thief, for he came to me not as a saint, but as a thief who stole my heart.

A FUNNY STORY ABOUT MY PET

Our pets bring us joy and laughter. Share a funny story about your pet in these pages.

A FUNNY STORY ABOUT MY PET

Use these pages to illustrate the comical nature of your animal friend.

MY FAVORITE STORY ABOUT YOU

Are There Potato Buns in Heaven?

Have you ever come home from work to discover that your pet has been lounging on the couch all day? Right before opening the door to the house I would hear a funny thud as my dog jumped from the couch. Ole Toby dog sat obediently erect to greet me as the door opened. His innocence stole my heart and always made me laugh. I'm sure Toby's cracked smile was his own amazing trick so that I only saw him as such a good dog!

One day as I was getting ready to leave for work I placed a full bag of potato buns at the far end of the counter. When I arrived home that evening, I realized that the potato buns were missing. There were no crumbs, no plastic bag, absolutely no evidence of Toby having been the one who consumed a whole bag of buns.

Weeks passed, and it was time to thoroughly clean the house. I lifted the couch cushion, and there was one whole bun. As I continued to clean, it was like an Easter egg hunt. I uncovered potato buns that had been hidden under pillows and blankets. Toby had even strategically placed a ration of buns under the bed. My imagination got the best of me for I could see Toby stretched out on the couch with a potato bun in paw, smile on his face, enjoying a snack.

Three weeks later, Toby got out of the front door and was hit and killed by a car. Two weeks after Toby's death I noticed a lumpy object in the middle of the driveway. I was shocked to find a bag of potato buns. It was Toby's sign to me that he had lived on.

MY FAVORITE STORY ABOUT YOU

Use these pages to tell one of your favorite stories about your pet.

HOW TO CELEBRATE
YOUR ANIMAL FRIEND'S LIFE

~

CHAPTER FOUR

HOW TO CELEBRATE YOUR ANIMAL FRIEND'S LIFE

CHAPTER FOUR

WAYS TO MEMORIALIZE YOUR ANIMAL

You can create a memorial service to honor and celebrate your pet's life. Creation of a ritual provides for healing and is a way to nurture your spirit.

You might enjoy and benefit from one of these choices:

• Have a special outing with your friends and family to scatter ashes.

• Plant roses, flowers, or a tree in memory of your pet.

• Give a donation to your favorite charity in memory of your pet.

• Purchase an animal book and give it to a child in memory of your pet.

• Give a donation to the many organizations that fund animal health research or the protection of the animal kingdom.

All of life is a ceremony.
–Jacqueline Kennedy

MY PET'S SPECIAL CEREMONY

If you had a special ceremonty for your pet, or would like to plan one, use these pages to describe the ceremony.

THE FUNERAL OF TREBLES THE CAT

I have been a minister for many years and still in my heart there remains a memory of one of the most profound funerals that I have ever experienced. Trebles had passed on into the greater continuum of life, and her owner had held her all night long. Before dawn the owner's dear friends and myself gathered and surrounded Trebles. Her body had stiffened through the night and was now wrapped in a soft blanket.

As the sun crested on the horizon, a drum beat; and with freshly picked wild flowers, sage, and sweet grass we sang as we carried Trebles to her final resting place in the field she had explored so many times before. I prayed, and Trebles' owner and her friends dug the earthen grave where Trebles' body would be cradled by Grandmother Earth. The sage smoke circled above as the grave was lined with flowers. Very slowly Trebles was lowered into her final resting place. We all placed the moist soil upon her now empty shell body.

Every time I drive by that beautiful field I think of the love that Trebles gave and the love she received as she journeyed up the earth.

Life is a journey and although
Our friends have gone
On without us, they
Live on in our hearts and minds,
Never forgotten.

EULOGY
FOR TREBLES

We have gathered at the most powerful time of day–dawn. As we stand in this dew-coated field, we feel the tears of our souls. I call upon the great energy of the seven directions of light. Grandmother Earth, as we prepare the earth to cradle Trebles, we give thanks for your life under our feet. To the sky we honor Grandfather, the source of all light and love.

To the east, the rising sun, I honor the newness of this day.
To the south, we feel great respect for all life, the mineral, the plants, the life within the sea, the four leggeds and the winged ones, and a blessing for all of humanity.

To the west we honor the power of change in our lives. It has come here today with big winds.
The north, I honor the place of stillness. Trebles' body is stilled in order for her soul to be right now a part of all life, the wind, the sun, the sky, and the Earth.

We know that Grandmother Earth holds the tiny robe of Trebles' soul safely. These freshly picked flowers now surround her bodily remains.

We will always be grateful for the love and the life of our precious animals. For the love of Trebles we sing "grateful, grateful" and release this one to the care and keeping of eternal life.

EULOGY
FOR ANDY

We honor the life of an angel.
Andy was adopted from a dog shelter. His previous owner had to give
Andy away because of recurring cancer that he could not manage.

The shelter permitted Christiana to send the previous owner a note to
say that she would take good care of his pet. Christiana had longed for
the companionship that only Andy could have provided. Andy was an
angel that assisted her to know great love. He was the reason that
love was born.

Andy was a blessing
for he was a strong and handsome German Shepherd angel.
It was Andy who lay by Christiana's side during the challenging times
of recovering from brain surgeries. It was Andy who stood at attention
while Christiana focused on living effectively moment by moment.
One day Christiana had a seizure. It was Andy
who found his way out the front door
and alerted a neighbor of Christiana's need.

Andy stayed long enough to kiss Christiana's baby boy
and to know that he too is an angel, "Miracle Boy."
Go now, my friend Andy, back to the meadow of heart. Play and be
young again. Shine your light through the heavens. Dear Andy, I
sense that in the day of tomorrow you will appear once again. In the
day of tomorrow my "Miracle Boy" will say,
"Mommy, Mommy look at this big fuzzy dog
that has found me."
Thank you Andy—Angel forever!

EULOGY FROM MY HEART

Write a heartfelt eulogy for your pet.

A TRIBUTE TO BEAU

Run Free Beau, Run Free

With the passing of Beau we knew immediately that we would have him cremated and scatter his ashes in a sacred place on the mountain where we had camped along with Maggie, our Border Collie. Why we chose this special place–now there is a story that needs to be told.

I had adopted Beau from an animal shelter. We were never sure if he had ever been on a camping trip before. His first night in the teepee he cried most of the night. He definitely did not want to sleep inside a teepee in the midst of the national forest. Six times that evening I had unlaced the teepee to take Beau outside; six times I had laced him back inside. I lay on my cot and offered a prayer to the Great Spirit that Beau would just settle down and be still and fall asleep in the cool mountain night.

Miracles do happen I thought, for he became still. I was ever so thankful. However, within moments of the blessed silence, I smelled a familiar barnyard smell. As my husband moved on his cot, his pillow slipped off and right into the fresh pile Beau had deposited on the floor.

For the seventh time the teepee was unlaced, and now my husband was taking Beau outside to spend the night. He tied Beau to an aspen tree where Beau slept safely and quietly the rest of the evening, in spite of bears that roam the forest. Now I prayed for protection for this big fuzzy dog as he sat on the hill and silently watched the stars overhead.

Morning came and Beau was rested and happy on the hill. So, when Beau died we knew we needed to take him to the hill where he so bravely quested under the starry sky.

When I found Beau dead at the foot of our bed, I held him and cried. I recall that I said to him, "Who will feed you now?" My second response was to pray and ask for guidance for the bear of a dog. We carefully placed him on a blanket and moved him outside where Maggie lay by his side.

I called the veterinarian, and my husband went to retrieve a friend to help lift old Beau into our truck for his final ride. As I left the house to accompany the two men and Beau, I gathered my special Pendleton blanket that my adopted Indian sister, Violet, had given me. I also took with me four sage ankle bracelets. Upon arriving at the animal hospital where I signed papers for the cremation of Beau's body, I asked the veternarian and his technician if I could place the sage bracelets on Beau's four legs and leave with Beau a braid of sweet grass. As I knelt to place the bracelets upon his legs I gave thanks for the world's biggest Airedale. I covered him with my sis's Pendleton blanket and the veterinarian assured me Beau would be cremated with the bracelets, sweet grass, and blanket. By fully participating, and ceremonially adorning Beau's body, the compassion of our veterinarian will always comfort my heart.

Scattering his ashes on the hill was harder than I anticipated. I cried as my husband spoke, "Run free, Beau, run free." His ashes blew in the gentle wind. I saluted the four directions of the Great Medicine Wheel and shared Beau's ashes with the earth. The remainder of his remains I placed within an earthen grave.

Now when we go to the mountain to spend the night in the teepee, I know that Beau is resting out on that hill in the moonlight.

ODE TO BEAU

In loving memory of the largest of all Airedales

There you were at the fair,
a big grandpa dog seeking a home.
You were the biggest clown I had ever seen.
You brought to mind my childhood fantasy,
a curly ragged dog to love and adore.
I remember the ride home with you in the car.
You were so big that your bottom was on the front seat
and your front legs touched the floor.
Your chin, pointing the way home, was on the dashboard.

You became Maggie's friend and my boy friend.
Mr. Beau Man, Cartoon, Mr. Man, you tickled my soul.
You lived to eat, and the morning I discovered your body,
so still in death, I cried, "Who will feed you now?"

I gave you a home, and you filled it with love.
You, dear friend, will always live in my heart.
If I could build a bridge to your soulful kingdom,
I would meet you there with yummy dog treats.
We could cuddle and court the stars in the night sky.

Your earthly remains will grace "Medicine Mountain,"
Right where you spent the night so freely and
bravely on the hill.

Thank you for finding me at the fair,
Mr. Beau Jingles Bear.
I'll see you on the mountain.

–Dr. Patty Luckenbach

ODE TO MY ANIMAL FRIEND

Write your own ode to your special animal friend.

WHEN YOU'RE READY TO RELEASE

CHAPTER FIVE

WHEN YOU'RE READY TO RELEASE

CHAPTER FIVE

FREE TO RELEASE, FREE TO REMEMBER

When are we ever ready to release our beloved pets? As time moves forward we find our emotional reaction to the loss of our pet erupting less frequently than it did when our pet first died. The love that was shared may be ready to be released in order for it to continue to be shared in our lives.

I share the story of a beautiful woman who had to make that difficult decision to put her pet to sleep. Her heart cried for months after his passing. After she gave herself permission to speak about her pain and to honor his life, she was able to speak fondly about him without the eruption of tears. She could even laugh and share funny stories about her friend.

Please know that you will know when it is time for you to place in the hallway of your heart your pet's name, because you will know that your pet lives forever within the kingdom of heart.

ONE LIFE

If we have wept for one life,
We see all life differently.
If we have wept for one mother, one child,
We see mothers and children differently.
If we have wept for one cat, one dog, one bird,
We see each of them anew.
Their preciousness, their uniqueness,
Emerges bathed clean in our tears.
One life is all life,
One child is all children,
One cat is all cats,
All life is one.
Would that it took not
Tears to open our eyes.

–Cinder Noor Ewanu DeField

I REMEMBER WHEN

What are your feelings about your pet? What memories are most precious to you? If you like, write some of your memories of your pet in the following pages. Our animal friends connect with our hearts, so let your emotions flow onto the paper.

HEART MEDITATION

I enter into the forest and into the jungle
and into the meadow of my mind.

Within my mind is the kingdom of heart,
and within this kingdom I seek to find the still point of my being.

Within this kingdom is a divine law
that is encoded within my very soul.
Deep, deep within is my instinctual kingdom.

The sounds of all of life call to me.
From above, so below, and all around about,
the harmonizing symphony of sound calms me.
I am one in this safe and all harmonizing feeling.

My inner wisdom is tuned.
I realize that all of life is connected,
and I am a part of it all.

I walk into the very center of this green and glorious forest of mind.
My heart can smell the sweetness of the wildflowers that grace the
meadow of my heart.

As I walk from the forest out
into the center of the meadow–there you are!

I call your name.
There we are, together in the very center of the meadow
of my heart.

Thank you for being in my life.

Thank you for trusting me and being my friend.

You will always live within my heart,
for we are forever one, for love is forever!

I can come to this place
within the kingdom of heart, anytime, anywhere.

We have a friendship that is forever.

When I need your presence beside me,
I will call your name.

When you need to rest and feel great love,
I will feel you curled and resting beside me.

Love is forever.

I NOW FEEL

If you would like to write about the love in your heart, or any other feeling, do so here.

Thy day has Come, not gone
Thy sun has Risen, not set
Thy life is new beyond the reach
Of death or change,
Not ended–but Begun.
O gentle heart!
Hail and farewell.

–W. S. Brain